Contents

Illustrators:
Steve Burgess pages 22-23
Barbara Firth pages 10-11, 24-25
Sean Milne pages 16-17
Dee Morgan pages 14-15, 18-19, 20-21,
    26-27
Clive Scruton pages 8-9
George Sharp pages 6-7, 42-43
Peter Snowball pages 28-29, 30-31,
    38-39, end sheets, title page, cover
Peter Visscher pages 36-37
David Wright pages 34-35, 40-41
Kathy Wyatt pages 12-13, 32-33

Editor: David Lloyd
Art editor: Pat Butterworth

Consultants: Chris Humphreys
                    Dan Freeman

First American edition published in 1984 by
Peter Bedrick Books
125 East 23 Street
New York, NY 10010
© 1983 Walker Books Ltd

Published by agreement with Walker Books Ltd, London.

Library of Congress Cataloguing in Publication Data
Bantock, Cuillin.
    The story of life.
    Includes index.
    Summary: Describes the creation and growth of all
life – human, plant, and animal.
    1. Life (Biology) – Juvenile literature. [1. Life
(Biology)] I. Title.
QH501.B36 1984   574   83-25730
ISBN 0-911745-51-3

Manufactured in Italy
Distributed in the USA by Harper & Row

To see a World in a Grain of Sand
And a Heaven in a Wild Flower,
Hold Infinity in the palm of your hand
And Eternity in an hour.

William Blake

THE STORY OF LIFE

Written by Cuillin Bantock

PETER BEDRICK BOOKS
NEW YORK

In the beginning

Every person on earth was once a baby, and every baby once had a body not much bigger than a grain of sand. This body had no arms or legs, no bones or muscles, no face to smile with. It was just a speck of chemicals called a cell. It could not see, hear, taste, touch or smell. But it was alive, and by its nature it knew something. It knew how to become a baby and what kind of baby to become.

Every living creature starts like this, as a single cell. A baby, a butterfly, a bird, a frog – each begins as a cell. Every dinosaur that ever lived began as a cell. So does every daffodil, dandelion and daisy.

The yolk of a chicken's egg is a cell. It looks nothing like a chicken, but in three weeks it can turn into one. A hen lays and incubates the egg. But only if the egg has been fertilised by a cockerel before it is laid will it later become a chick.

A man makes love with a woman and releases into her body many millions of sperm. Each sperm is a cell, but with only half the knowledge of how to become a baby. The woman makes an ovum, a cell with the other half. Just one sperm has to join with the ovum to make the complete cell from which a new person begins.

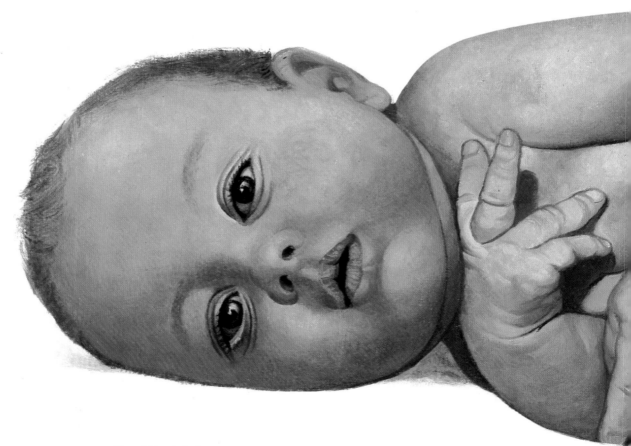

How old is a baby?

Every baby has parents, and all parents were once babies themselves, with parents of their own. Life can come only from life. No one can say exactly how long life has existed on earth, but perhaps it is as many as 4,000 million years. A baby, naked and helpless, is new to the world. But also it is as old as life itself.

The sperm joins with the ovum inside the woman's body, in warmth, safety and darkness. In the first moment of its existence the microscopic living cell already contains enough information to fill thousands of books.

If the books could ever be written they would describe in great detail the person whose life is beginning, the colour of eyes, hair and skin, the shape of fingers, toes, nose and ears. All this knowledge exists in the genes of the cell, the master chemicals of life.

Years later, when the cell has become a baby and the baby has grown into a child, the child may smile and someone may say: 'When you smile, you look just like your mother.' This way of smiling, this look, also existed there in the genes of the cell, from the instant of its beginning.

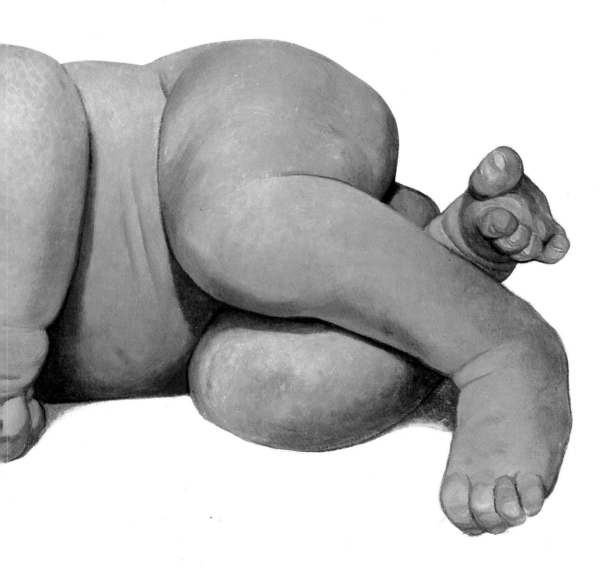

Power plant

Waste disposal

Directors' office

Assembly

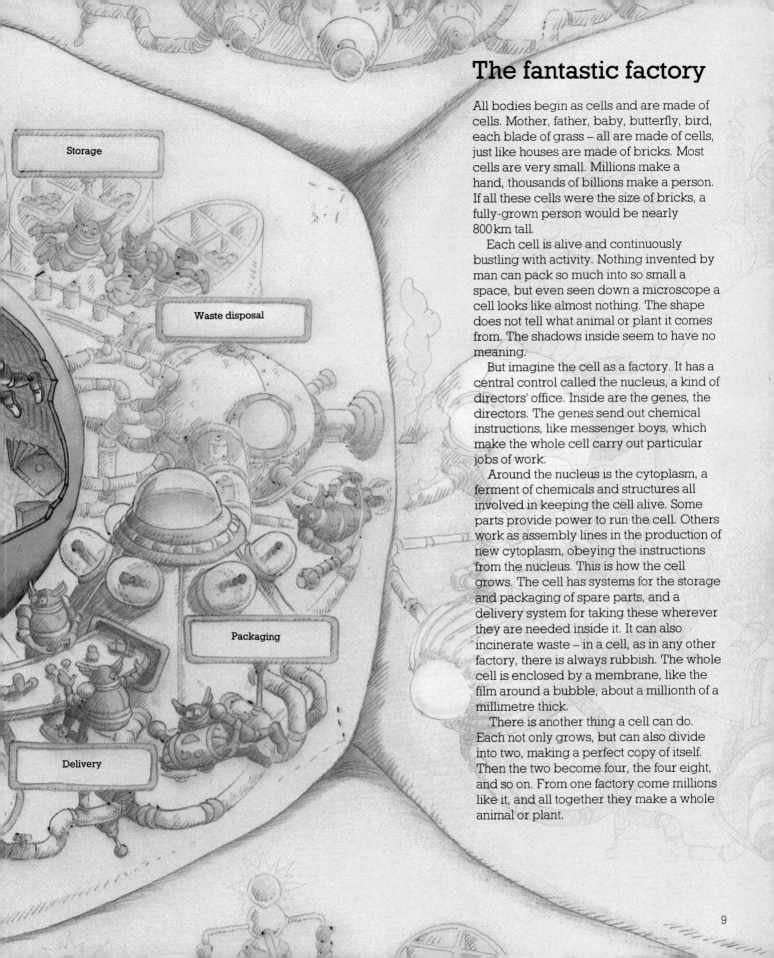

The fantastic factory

All bodies begin as cells and are made of cells. Mother, father, baby, butterfly, bird, each blade of grass – all are made of cells, just like houses are made of bricks. Most cells are very small. Millions make a hand, thousands of billions make a person. If all these cells were the size of bricks, a fully-grown person would be nearly 800 km tall.

Each cell is alive and continuously bustling with activity. Nothing invented by man can pack so much into so small a space, but even seen down a microscope a cell looks like almost nothing. The shape does not tell what animal or plant it comes from. The shadows inside seem to have no meaning.

But imagine the cell as a factory. It has a central control called the nucleus, a kind of directors' office. Inside are the genes, the directors. The genes send out chemical instructions, like messenger boys, which make the whole cell carry out particular jobs of work.

Around the nucleus is the cytoplasm, a ferment of chemicals and structures all involved in keeping the cell alive. Some parts provide power to run the cell. Others work as assembly lines in the production of new cytoplasm, obeying the instructions from the nucleus. This is how the cell grows. The cell has systems for the storage and packaging of spare parts, and a delivery system for taking these wherever they are needed inside it. It can also incinerate waste – in a cell, as in any other factory, there is always rubbish. The whole cell is enclosed by a membrane, like the film around a bubble, about a millionth of a millimetre thick.

There is another thing a cell can do. Each not only grows, but can also divide into two, making a perfect copy of itself. Then the two become four, the four eight, and so on. From one factory come millions like it, and all together they make a whole animal or plant.

Storage

Waste disposal

Packaging

Delivery

One plus one

A single cell becomes a baby and the baby grows up. A seed falls on the ground and turns into a plant, complete with flowers. A puppy becomes a dog, a tadpole becomes a frog, a gaping nestling becomes an owl hooting in the night. A cut finger heals. All this is possible because each cell can grow and reproduce itself by dividing into two.

Inside the nucleus of every cell are its genes, which are carried on threads called chromosomes. Every human cell has 23 pairs of chromosomes, one set of 23 brought by the sperm, the other by the ovum. A frog has 22 pairs, a kangaroo 6 pairs, a daffodil 7 pairs. In each case the genes carry information unique to the life they are making. The first cell divides, the new cells divide, something grows – a frog, a kangaroo or a person, whatever the genes dictate.

Before a cell divides, its chromosomes double. The nuclear membrane is absorbed into the cytoplasm. Half the chromosomes move to one end of the cell

and half to the other. The cell tightens round the middle and eventually divides into two. Each of the two new cells has a nucleus containing the original number of chromosomes. The genes continue to direct. The process of growth and division starts again.

Cells are the smallest things that can live on their own. In a drop of pondwater or a pinch of garden soil, there may be hundreds of minute plants and animals, all of which have bodies made of only one cell. In spite of being so simple, they can do all that is necessary to stay alive. Most important of all, they can reproduce. The one-celled body divides, and one plant or animal becomes two. Each is the same as the other, like identical twins. These are among the oldest forms of life on earth.

The process of cell division has been going on since life first began on earth. Cells come only from other cells, life comes only from life, parents are just children who grew up and had children.

Diatom
There are many different sorts of these plants, which often stick together in groups.

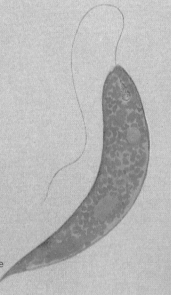

Euglena
Part plant, part animal, which can eat and also use sunlight to make food.

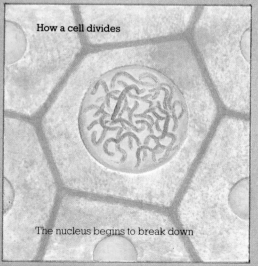

How a cell divides

The nucleus begins to break down

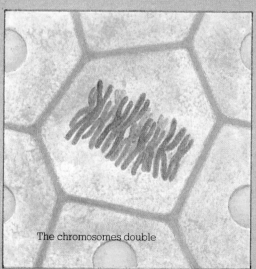

The chromosomes double

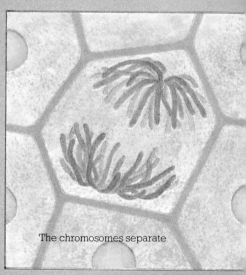

The chromosomes separate

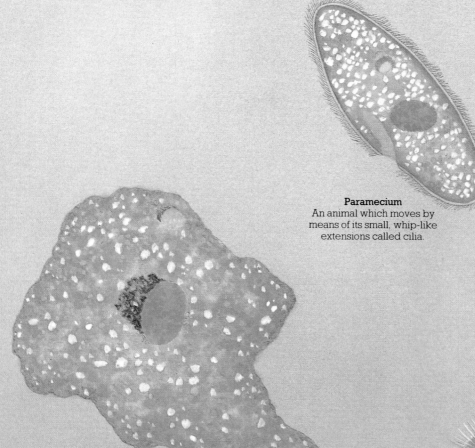

Paramecium
An animal which moves by means of its small, whip-like extensions called cilia.

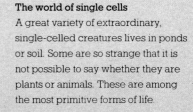

The world of single cells
A great variety of extraordinary, single-celled creatures lives in ponds or soil. Some are so strange that it is not possible to say whether they are plants or animals. These are among the most primitive forms of life.

Amoeba
An animal which creeps over mud, constantly changing shape.

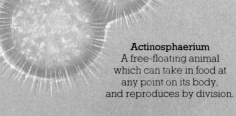

Actinosphaerium
A free-floating animal which can take in food at any point on its body, and reproduces by division.

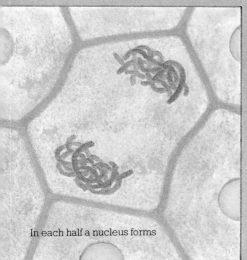

In each half a nucleus forms

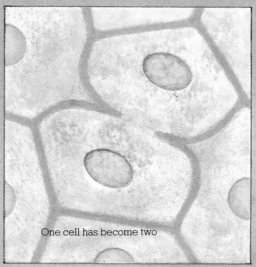

One cell has become two

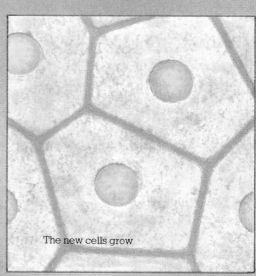

The new cells grow

Life before birth

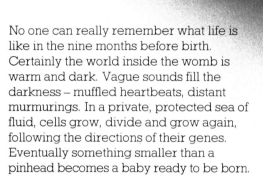

No one can really remember what life is like in the nine months before birth. Certainly the world inside the womb is warm and dark. Vague sounds fill the darkness – muffled heartbeats, distant murmurings. In a private, protected sea of fluid, cells grow, divide and grow again, following the directions of their genes. Eventually something smaller than a pinhead becomes a baby ready to be born.

It is in the first two months that the foetus develops most rapidly. At first it looks similar to the foetus of a dog, a rabbit or almost any kind of animal. For a while it seems to have gills like a fish, and for several weeks it even has a tail. At four weeks old it is about the size of a grain of rice, but already blind swellings mark the beginnings of eyes, and inside the worm-like body a tiny heart is already beating. By the seventh week the baby is clearly human, but only an inch long.

Mother and baby have separate hearts and separate blood streams, but the mother eats, digests and breathes for the baby, and clears out through her body all the baby's waste. A life-support system called the placenta develops in the womb, and the baby is attached to it by its umbilical cord. In the placenta only the finest layer of cells separates the baby's blood stream from the mother's. Through this passes everything the baby needs, carried in the mother's blood stream to the placenta, and then from the placenta to the baby's blood stream through the umbilical cord.

The months of pregnancy are a meticulous preparation for free life. They end with one of the toughest tests of all – birth, the sudden change from privacy and shelter to the bright, uncertain world outside. The umbilical cord attaching the baby to the placenta is cut. Never again in a lifetime will so many drastic changes happen all at once.

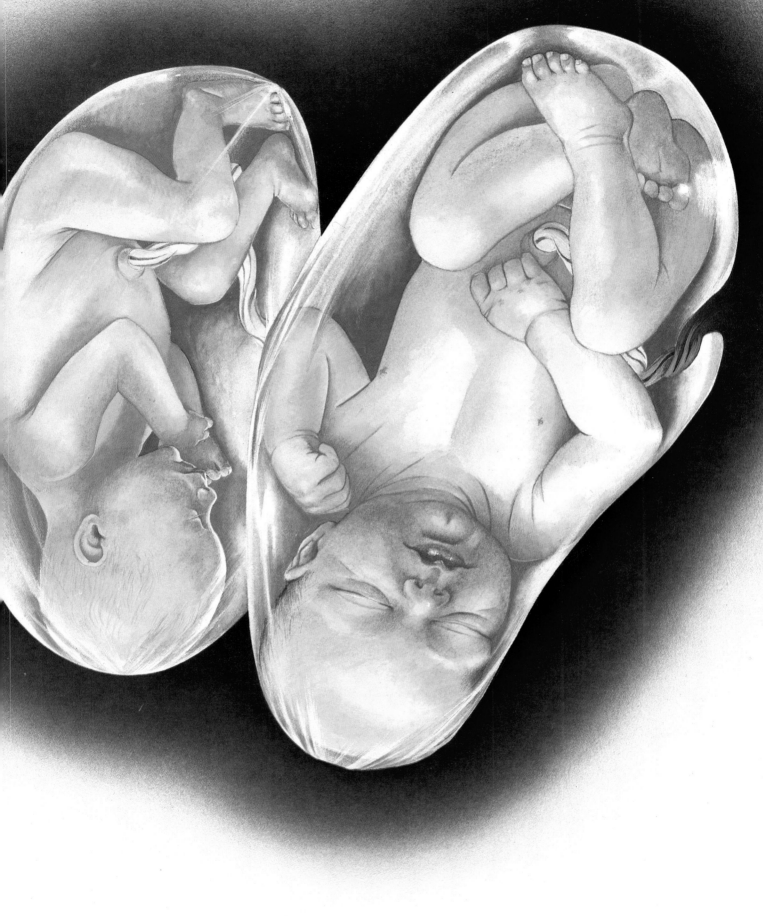

Going on

Eggs

Peacock butterfly

All forms of life have a tremendous urge to survive. GO ON is a rule that applies to all, go on in any way that works. There are many ways. Every kind of plant or animal has a special way of its own.

The peacock butterfly starts life in spring, as a single cell in a tiny capsule abandoned by the female on a nettle leaf. The cell grows into a caterpillar, which bites its way out of the capsule. It is surrounded by other caterpillars, all its brothers and sisters. Each is so small that a single drop of dew may drown it. If the sun is too hot, it shrivels and dies. If the air is too damp, it is attacked by fungus and dies.

The caterpillars are defenceless in many ways, but they have large jaws and huge appetites. They eat the nettle and grow. They turn black and develop bristles and pearly warts. The writhing mass of caterpillars can be seen from several metres. No bird dares attack this object, but some of the family fall prey to wasps, which are less easily deceived by appearances.

The survivors grow until each is large enough to appear unappetising even on its

Fully-grown caterpillars

own. They then change into pupae. Some hang upside down on the nettle, others hang on trees. They look like green or brown leaves, motionless among real leaves. If they are seen, they get eaten.

In late summer the adult butterflies ease their way out of the pupae. With wings closed, they can hardly be seen against the bark of trees. If a bird spots one, the butterfly flicks its wings open, flashing the markings like eyes. The bird backs away, seeing the threatening eyes of an owl.

The butterflies feed throughout autumn, preparing for hibernation. For the six months of winter they hardly move, hidden in the cracks of trees and in other crevices. Some are eaten by mice.

Spring comes and the butterflies begin the last part of their lives. Sunshine warms their bedraggled wings. Males and females find one another and mate. The females lay their eggs on nettle leaves. Soon both males and females die.

But their eggs hatch, carrying life on into another generation. Going on is all that matters, for a butterfly or a baby, going on in the way that works for it.

Pupa

Peacock butterfly
emerging from pupa

15

Peacock butterfly

The owl machine

Tawny owl

There is a world of difference between the 'eyes' on the wings of a peacock butterfly and the real eyes of an owl. At a quick glance they look a bit alike, which may sometimes save the butterfly's life. But there the likeness ends. The butterfly's 'eyes' equip it to escape by day. The owl's eyes enable it to hunt by night. The butterfly can never kill like the owl, any more than the owl can suck nectar from flowers like the butterfly. Each is like a machine, which can work only in one way.

As daylight fades and night begins, an owl comes out from its daytime roosting place. It flies so quietly it seems to be floating on the air. Wherever it goes it is alert for the tiniest movement or the slightest rustle. Every detail of its body makes it a supreme hunting machine, ready at any moment to strike and kill.

Each of the owl's eyes is like a cine-camera. The eyes face forwards, set on prominent cylinders of bone. As the owl scans the ground, each eye sends a separate picture of the same scene back to the brain. The difference between the pictures tells the owl how far away everything is. The eyes are as big as a man's, and a hundred times more efficient.

The ears are like microphones, invisible, vertical slits on either side of the head. A shallow saucer of feathers around each reflects the sound inwards. One ear is higher than the other, making a tiny difference between the time any sound takes to reach them. The owl can tell from this where the slightest squeak or whisper came from. Just by listening, an owl can pinpoint and strike a frog even in complete darkness.

The night is quiet, so the hunting owl must make no noise. Under the feathers its body is lean and thin. The wings are light, the owl moves as silently as a huge moth. Even when it swerves in to strike, the edges of the wing feathers are so soft that there is no warning rush of air.

The claws are the striking weapons. One toe on each foot can turn backwards or forwards, to capture different kinds of prey. Songbirds, mice, snakes, frogs and beetles are all food for an owl. The narrow, down-curved beak is made for ripping and tearing their bodies.

The owl can live only by hunting. It cannot swim, dive or even peck in the ground. Like every living creature, it is adapted to one way of life. Its adaptations make it what it is, an owl and nothing else. Throughout nature, the differences between bodies make the differences between lives. Bodies never give their owners any choice.

Common frog

The owl's eyes
An owl's eyes are so large that they leave no room for eye muscles. An owl cannot move its eyes. Instead it can turn its head right round. Because the eyes are set well forward, there is a wide overlap (coloured dark blue in the diagram above) between what each eye can see. This allows the owl to judge distances accurately.

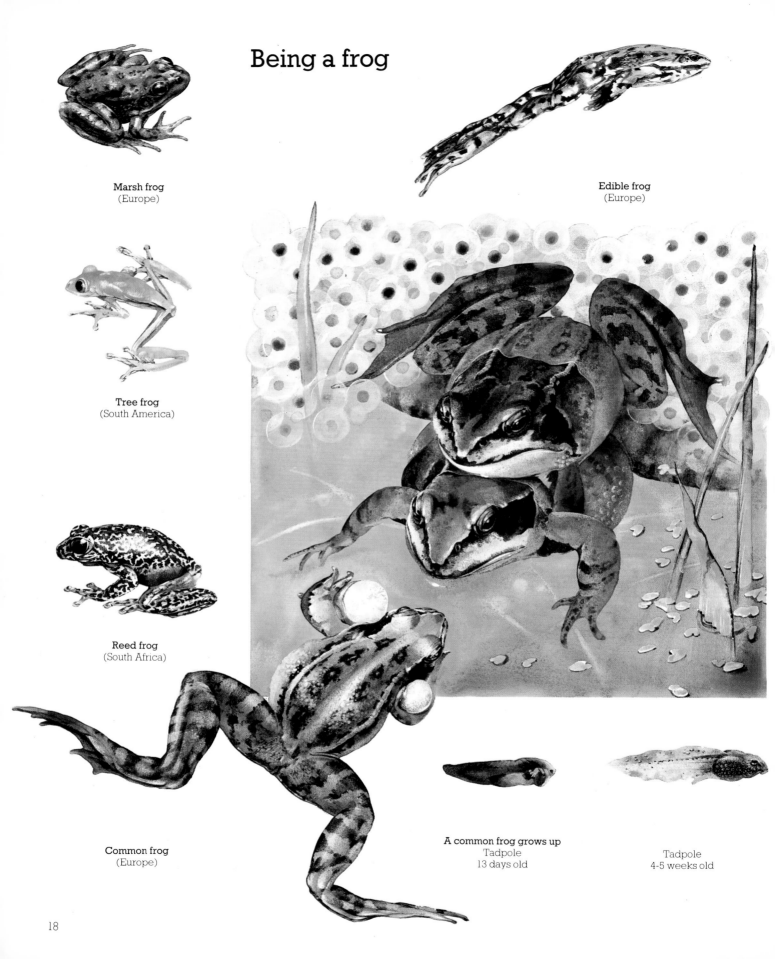

Being a frog

Marsh frog
(Europe)

Edible frog
(Europe)

Tree frog
(South America)

Reed frog
(South Africa)

Common frog
(Europe)

A common frog grows up
Tadpole
13 days old

Tadpole
4-5 weeks old

Tree frog
(Australia)

Chorus frog
(North America)

Flying frog
(South America)

Spotted poison arrow frog
(South America)

Every kind of animal or plant has something different about it, something which helps it to survive in its own special way. Every individual breeds only with another of its own kind. A tawny owl breeds only with a tawny owl, a common frog only with a common frog. In this way each species passes on its adaptations, the unique machinery of its body, from generation to generation. A common frog may die, eaten by an owl, a heron or a pike. But reproduction makes it possible for the common frog as a species to go on living just as long as the world remains a suitable place for frogs to live in. Already frogs have lived on earth for at least 100 million years.

The cheeks in a male common frog are like sheets of elastic. He can blow them out into balloons as big as his head. When he lets his breath go, the balloons collapse and he croaks. The croak of the common frog is unique. No other sound in nature is quite like it. It is the male's mating call, his song for a female of his own kind. In spring, the sound of males croaking from a pond can be heard from a hundred metres away. Soon the females come to join them.

The frogs mate in the water, each male staying clasped on the back of a female for several days. When both are ready, the female sheds a mass of eggs and the male squirts sperm cells over them. In seconds jelly swells around each egg. The black speck in the jelly is a common frog of the future, a single fertile cell ready to divide according to its genes.

There are some 2,600 species of frogs on earth, most of them living in tropical jungles. Each has a different mating call. In the mating season, the jungle resounds with a chorus of trills, snores, wet explosions, barks, burps and wails. Each female frog responds to the call of her own species, and to no other. The males of some species croak so hard that at first they do not notice when a female arrives. She nudges him to let him know she's there.

Frogspawn grows into tadpoles, which grow in turn into frogs. However many changes the frog goes through in its lifetime, the genes in its cells remain the same. The genes keep each species unique – different from all the others, the singer of a different song.

Poison arrow frog
(South America)

Tadpole
9 weeks old

Froglet
11 weeks old

Common frog
Adult

A swarm of sisters

With a tongue like instant flypaper, a frog licks an aphid out of the air and swallows it. An aphid is not much to eat or much to look at. It is only about 2mm long, and so frail that the slightest touch with your finger will crush it. And yet it has one great strength – the speed at which it can reproduce. Sometimes, in the summer, such vast families of aphids swarm into the air that they almost blot out the sun.

In spring, when aphid eggs hatch, all the aphids born are females. Within days these females give birth to other females, without mating with a male. Each generation is born with the next generation already growing inside it. Daughters become mothers almost as soon as they are born, and grandmothers as quickly afterwards. In a life lasting two to three weeks, each female has about 50 daughters – all of them breeding machines exactly like their mother.

By the summer, a single swarm which has come from one small group of females can number 800 million. This is when farmers and gardeners must watch out. The insects can do tremendous damage, infesting all sorts of plants and sucking out their juices with mouths like drinking straws.

When the first frost comes, all the aphids die. The population crashes to nothing. But shortly before, something important happens. Some males are born, which mate with some of the females. Before the frost these females lay eggs, tough enough to survive the winter. The aphids die, but their eggs lie safely on the leaves of trees and shrubs, waiting for the spring.

In nature, families come in all sizes. Aphids, frogs and butterflies have huge families, and most take no obvious care of them. Other animals have very few young and look after them in every possible way. But all species have more young than survive to a breeding age – in fact, all have just enough young to keep the number of adults the same from generation to generation. Life's urge to increase is like a fire, always capable of flaring up. But there is only so much of everything on earth – so much space, so much food, so much sunshine. For aphids, the killer frost always comes. Their eggs are safe, but their numbers are kept in check.

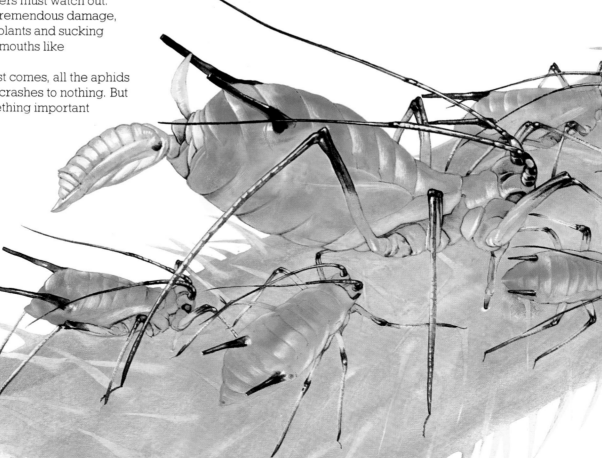

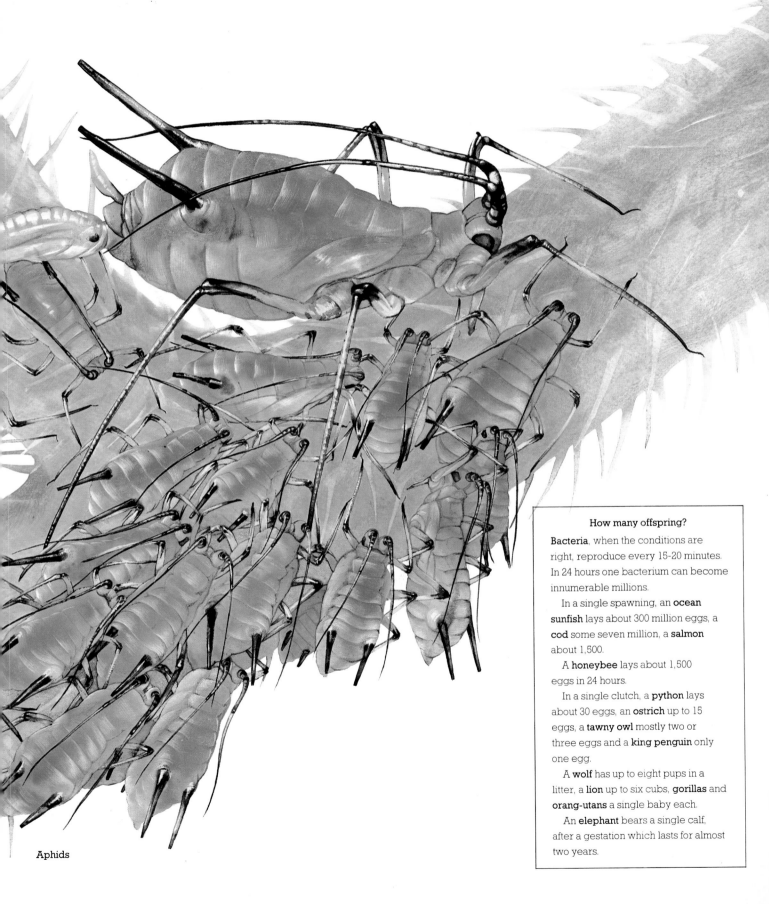

Aphids

How many offspring?

Bacteria, when the conditions are right, reproduce every 15-20 minutes. In 24 hours one bacterium can become innumerable millions.

In a single spawning, an **ocean sunfish** lays about 300 million eggs, a **cod** some seven million, a **salmon** about 1,500.

A **honeybee** lays about 1,500 eggs in 24 hours.

In a single clutch, a **python** lays about 30 eggs, an **ostrich** up to 15 eggs, a **tawny owl** mostly two or three eggs and a **king penguin** only one egg.

A **wolf** has up to eight pups in a litter, a **lion** up to six cubs, **gorillas** and **orang-utans** a single baby each.

An **elephant** bears a single calf, after a gestation which lasts for almost two years.

Only one you

Human beings look after their children longer than any other creature on earth. For years they guard them, guide them, play with them and provide for them. The lesson is quickly learnt that all children are different from each other.

You are very special. Your eyes, nose, hands, hair, skin, voice, frown, smile – every part of you is unique. And yet someone may say you smile just like your mother or look just like your father. Everyone always looks for family likenesses. They are one of the first things people always point out about babies.

In each of the billions of cells which make your body lies the store of genes inherited from your parents. From the moment you began, these determined whether you would be fair or dark, tall or short, blue-eyed or brown-eyed. In every person the combination of genes is different.

But your genetic make-up is more like your parents' than that of a friend. The genes came from your parents. The sperm brought genes from your father, the ovum brought genes from your mother. When a

sperm or an ovum first develops, genes are dealt to it from all the genes in that man or woman's body, like cards from a pack. There are so many genes that every sperm and ovum receives a different deal.

This is why a brother and sister are different from each other, and why they also have family likenesses. Each received a different deal from the same two packs. It also explains why a friend doesn't look like you at all. The friend's deal came from different packs.

In all creatures whose lives begin with the meeting between sperm and ovum, there will be differences between individuals. No two common frogs or tawny owls are exactly alike, though it may be hard for us to see any difference. But sister aphids born in the summer are identical. No mating occurred before they were born.

Sexual reproduction is important because of the differences it makes, because it makes individuals special. Because of the way you began, when a man and a woman made love, you are the only one you for ever.

A little difference

Animal and plant families are always too large for all the offspring to survive. The differences between individuals can be a matter of life or death. One frog lives and breeds, its brother does not. Perhaps the one that lived to breed was darker, less easy for an owl to see. Some of its young will also be dark, inheriting the genes for that colour. Such little differences, inherited through many generations, can change the whole species. In time it may come to be a different kind of animal altogether.

The wings of male ghost moths vary in colour from gleaming white to dull brown. The males have a strange, swaying flight, hardly moving over the ground. On still, summer evenings, they float over fields and meadows, ready to mate. The females come to the males, finding them by sight.

In the Shetland Islands, far to the north of Scotland, it is never really dark in summer. The females can see all the males, whatever colour their wings are. Further south, on the British mainland, the night comes earlier. Males with brown wings have never had much chance of being seen. Only the palest moths have left descendants. The genes which are passed on are those which make the whitest wings.

Pale wings show up in the dark and brown wings in the light. What works well in one place may be useless in another. But all ghost moths, whatever they look like, belong to the same species. Any two can breed together, if the opportunity occurs, to make another generation.

Male
ghost moths

Female
ghost moth

Male
ghost moths

Female
ghost moth

Basking in the sun

The green-veined white butterfly
basks in the sun to warm the blood in
its wing veins. Without warmth it
cannot reproduce.

On high mountains, where there is
little warmth, the butterflies have dark
veins. Dark colours absorb heat more
efficiently than pale ones. In warmer
places the wing veins are paler.

In Sweden, pale and dark-veined
butterflies breed together where they
meet on mountain slopes. But in the
southern Swiss Alps, the dark
butterflies are so isolated, and they
have changed so much adapting to
the cold, that they have almost
become a different species.

Winning ways

Frog to frog, moth to moth, man to woman – each species keeps its genes to itself. Each is like a separate island. Two species of animals cannot become one. But if some individuals of a species are isolated from the rest, by mountains, sea or any other barrier, they can become an island of genes on their own. In time they can change so much that they can no longer breed with near relatives in other places. Then one species has become two.

The shuffling of genes makes all individuals unique. The genes themselves stay the same, but the mixture varies. But there are also forces in nature powerful enough to change genes, producing new ones from old. The sun can do this – it does it all the time. These changes are random and accidental. Most of them are harmful. But occasionally a change occurs which helps an individual. This is the unexpected joker in the pack. These changes are the source of all new variation.

Only the best-adapted individuals have descendants. Only the palest ghost moths survive in England, only the darkest green-veined whites lay eggs in the Alps.

A fish that fishes
The angler fish looks like part of the sea-bed, with a worm wriggling in front of it. The worm is part of its body, a lure to attract its prey.

Back to front
Disturb this lantern-fly and it seems to jump backwards. What looks like its head is really part of its wings. The true head is at the other end.

A drop of dew
Resting on a leaf, a tortoise beetle from the forests of Borneo looks like a drop of dew. Its body is gold, but the wings are transparent.

This weeding-out process, called natural selection, goes on all the time, in every species, everywhere.

In spring male bumble bees leave their underground burrows to search for mates. But the females stay underground for another two weeks. A plant, the bee orchid, benefits from this. The female part of the flower has to receive pollen from a male part before it can set seed, to produce the next generation. On each flower a large, furry petal looks like a female bee. The male bee flies from flower to flower, attracted by the petals. Without knowing it, he transfers pollen from one to another. Only the orchids which look most like bees get pollinated and have offspring.

No two species can become one. But by natural selection one species can come to look like another. Or it can come to look like something else altogether. There are insects which look like leaves, fish which look like rocks, beetles which look like drops of dew. Disguise is a well-tried method of survival. In nature things are often not at all what they appear to be.

Fallen leaves which fly away
In tropical forests every leaf or flower may really be something else. This fallen leaf is a butterfly, ready to hop away at any moment.

Deceiving bees
The largest petal of a bee orchid looks just like a bee. Real bees are deceived into visiting it, and unconsciously help the flower to breed.

The killer killed

Deinonychus

Sabrefoot, terrible claw, deinonychus – under any name it remains one of the most blood-chilling beasts that ever lived on earth. It was a reptile, a lean killer dinosaur hardly taller than a man. It lived by butchery. One toe on each hind foot was different from the rest. It had a huge claw, a vicious, curved blade. Deinonychus attacked, clung to its prey, grappled. It used its claws like sickles, slitting open the bellies of other reptiles.

This nightmare creature was exactly suited to its world. It was just one of hundreds of species of reptile alive 80 million years ago. Some were enormous, the biggest land animals ever known. But just as butterflies have to absorb the sun's heat each day, so did these reptiles. They ruled the world for about 150 million years, but only during the day.

Every evening, as the sun set on their paradise of succulent ferns, clubmosses and giant horsetails, the reptiles cooled down, slowed down and slept. Deinonychus may have just stood still in the dark, waiting for the sun to rise again.

Over enormous periods of time the world changes. Land and sea change places, mountains rise and wear away, deserts replace forests. The climate may be anything from baking hot to freezing. As the world changes, living creatures must change too. If they do not, they become extinct, however common they once were.

Some 65 million years ago, the sun set for ever for the dinosaurs. Within a relatively short time every species became extinct. There are many theories why this happened. Perhaps the climate became too cold. Perhaps the plant-life changed, and the plant-eaters could no longer eat it. If the plant-eaters died, so would the meat-eaters like deinonychus, which preyed on them. No one knows which of all the theories is right.

Somehow the world changed and the dinosaurs were left behind, victims of their adaptations. Deinonychus, brontosaurus, tyrannosaurus rex – all died out. Their bodies washed down mountain gorges in the rains and rotted away. Some of their bones, whitening in river beds, became fossils. The world was never the same again.

A claw in stone

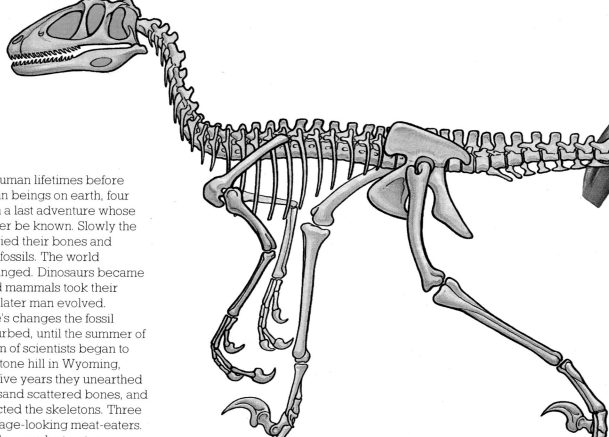

About a million human lifetimes before there were human beings on earth, four dinosaurs died in a last adventure whose full story will never be known. Slowly the shifting earth buried their bones and turned them into fossils. The world changed, life changed. Dinosaurs became extinct, birds and mammals took their place, and much later man evolved.

Through all life's changes the fossil bones lay undisturbed, until the summer of 1964, when a team of scientists began to excavate a sandstone hill in Wyoming, USA. In the next five years they unearthed more than a thousand scattered bones, and slowly reconstructed the skeletons. Three of them were savage-looking meat-eaters. The fourth was a larger plant-eater, perhaps the prey of the other three. The scientists had discovered deinonychus, the dinosaur which killed with the claws on its feet.

It will never be known what colour skin deinonychus had, what its flesh was like, or what sort of sounds it made. Fossil bones are all that is left of it, the only evidence that it existed at all. The skeletons are incomplete. The tops of the skulls were never found, nor were the thigh bones or many of the ribs or bones in the back.

Altogether there are about six million species of plants and animals known only from their fossilised remains – many more than there are species alive on earth today. Trying to tell the story of how they lived and died, changed or became extinct, is like doing a jigsaw puzzle when you don't know what the picture is, and when many of the pieces are missing.

If all the bodies of all the animals that have ever lived were displayed in some colossal and fantastic museum, and if you yourself could live long enough to look at all the exhibits, it would be possible to see how all life's changes have taken place. How fish came out of the sea to live on the land, how reptiles became birds, how human beings evolved – all this would become clear. As it is, fossils tell only a small fraction of the story. For the rest, scientists can only make theories about how things really happened.

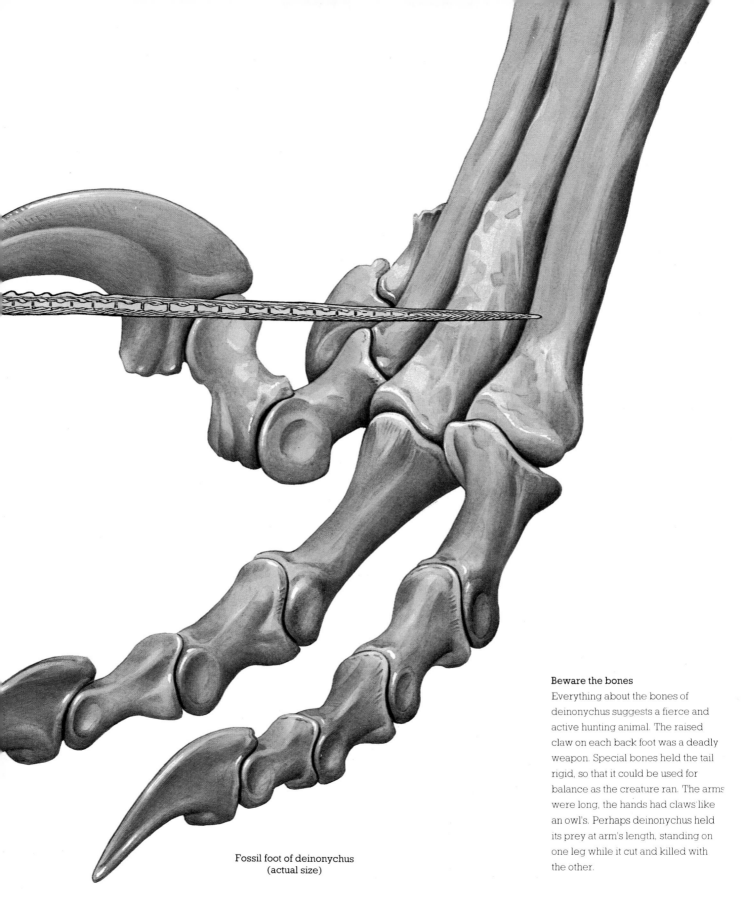

Fossil foot of deinonychus
(actual size)

Beware the bones

Everything about the bones of deinonychus suggests a fierce and active hunting animal. The raised claw on each back foot was a deadly weapon. Special bones held the tail rigid, so that it could be used for balance as the creature ran. The arms were long, the hands had claws like an owl's. Perhaps deinonychus held its prey at arm's length, standing on one leg while it cut and killed with the other.

People before people

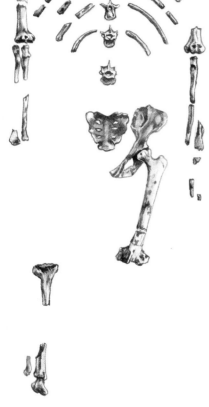

As the dinosaurs died out, small, shrew-like creatures may have been darting about close beside them, looking for insects and fruit to eat. They had long muzzles and sharp teeth, and fed mainly at night. In time their eyes came to be set well to the front of their heads, giving the accurate vision needed for life in trees. These may have been the ancestors of a group of animals called the primates. If so, their descendants were to inherit the earth. For the primate who has now overrun the earth is man.

It took some 70 million years for descendants of the animals that saw the end of the dinosaurs to evolve into modern man. There is no simple way of saying how this happened. The fossil evidence is fragmentary, and different people link the fragments in different ways. The true history of human evolution will probably always be a subject for argument.

By comparing human beings with other living animals, it is clear that the animals on earth most like us are gorillas and chimpanzees. Long ago we may all have been members of the same species. Already, by natural selection, these animals had changed almost beyond recognition from their far-off ancestors.

Ape-like animals called ramapithecus lived in Africa some 13 million years ago. It seems likely, from studying the fossils, that they lived on the ground and fed at least partly on plants. They may also have walked upright. Living in grassland and scrub instead of in trees, apes walking on two legs would have been the most alert to danger and the most likely to survive. They could also have used their arms and hands for something other than moving from place to place.

The first man-like animals to use tools were probably australopithecus, which lived some five million years ago. With crude pieces of wood or stone, or even broken bones, they cut plants or killed other animals to eat. The habit was copied and elaborated. Later ancestors began sharpening stones, at first on one side, then on both. It was only a matter of time before the axe was invented. The urge to make things and to change the world is one of the features that most clearly distinguishes modern man from his most distant ancestors, and from the rest of the animal kingdom.

By some means the shrews became apes and apes human beings. By 50,000 years ago the world was becoming increasingly settled by people physically very similar to people today. They walked upright, had high domed foreheads shielding fully-developed brains, knew how to use fire, drew pictures on the walls of their caves. Much has changed since then in the way we live and the tools we use. But our appearance has hardly changed at all.

Lucy
The fossil bones of a three million-year-old australopithecine, probably female, were found in Ethiopia in 1974. She was nicknamed Lucy.

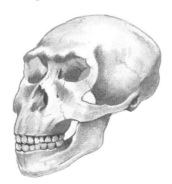

Handy man
Homo habilus, which means handy man, lived a little less than two million years ago. Habilines were among the earliest creatures to make and use tools.

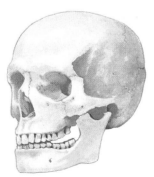

Wise man
People today are called Homo sapiens, which means wise man. Our skulls show that we have large brains, like our early ancestor, handy man.

Tree and leaf

Eight months before a baby is born, a small bud of dividing cells appears on each side of its body. The buds slowly develop into arms. First the upper arm appears, then the forearm grows, last come the wrist, palm, fingers and thumb. The thumb can touch the fingers end to end. No other animal on earth can do this. Because of the way your thumb moves, you can do all sorts of things unique to human life.

About two hundred other species have hands. Chimpanzee hands are the most like our own, though they cannot perform such delicate tasks. A larger number of animals have forelimbs designed like the human arm, but without hands. A bat's long finger bones support its dark wing membrane. A whale has similar bones arranged close together inside its flippers.

Each kind of animal is like a leaf on a tree. Two leaves close together are species which are very similar, like humans and chimpanzees. Leaves on different twigs but on the same branch are species with much in common, but also with major differences. Humans and fish are on the same branch, because both have backbones.

Animals without backbones, including insects and other creatures whose bodies are inside their skeletons, make another branch. Insects have legs, but they are built in a very different way to the legs of backboned animals. In insects, the design of the limbs is similar to that of some of the first large sea animals, which lived some 500 million years ago.

Plants also make a separate branch. Plants and animals are very different, but both are made of cells. And for both, the fossil record always leads back to life in the water, and eventually to single-celled species living in the sea.

Many scientists believe that the tree has branched and grown its leaves by slow evolution, with natural selection causing one species gradually to change into another. The hardest question of all is where cells came from in the first place, how the seed from which the tree grew ever came to be sown.

Tortoise

Plants

Norway spruce

Bluebell

Bracken

Green algae

Moss

Lichen

Fly agaric

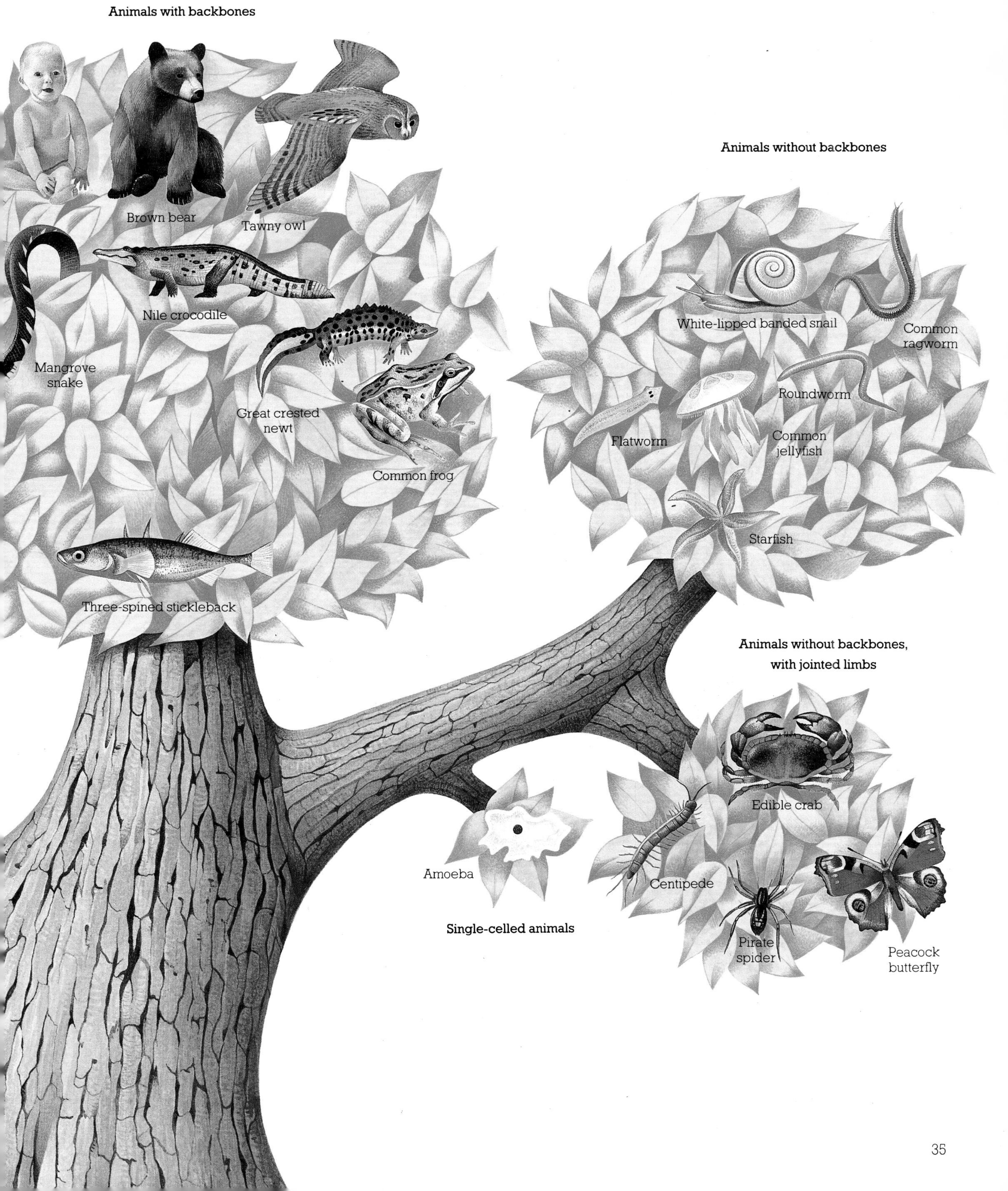

Animals with backbones

Brown bear

Tawny owl

Nile crocodile

Mangrove
snake

Great crested
newt

Common frog

Three-spined stickleback

Animals without backbones

White-lipped banded snail

Common
ragworm

Roundworm

Flatworm

Common
jellyfish

Starfish

Animals without backbones,
with jointed limbs

Edible crab

Amoeba

Centipede

Single-celled animals

Pirate
spider

Peacock
butterfly

The combination mystery

A cell is a marvellously complicated combination of chemicals, but the simple elements from which these are combined – chiefly carbon, hydrogen, nitrogen and oxygen – exist everywhere in the sea, in rocks and in the air. In a cell the chemicals interact in a particular way, so that the interaction goes on and on. Life, for all its wonders and mysteries, is a chemical process whose raw materials already existed at the earth's creation.

The earth was born some 450 thousand million years ago, from a hot, swirling cloud of gas and dust. The cloud cooled, condensing to liquid with a crust all round it. Rain began to fall. Volcanic eruptions tore open the crust, leaving clouds of gas hanging over the steaming rock. The rain fell for centuries, making warm seas and filling them with chemicals washed from the rocks and out of the air.

Electric storms raged and the sun poured ultra-violet rays on to the newborn planet. The chemicals in the sea began to mix, making increasingly complex combinations. In still water, perhaps in rock pools sheltered from the worst of the storms, the combinations persisted for the longest time. Perhaps it was here that the chemicals first came together to make droplets capable of reproducing themselves. Only when the combination could recreate itself could it truly be called alive.

The first living cell was not born, it happened by chance. It may never be known how, or how long it took. The story can only be a theory. At some point a membrane surrounded the cell, controlling the entry of chemicals from outside. Other chemicals, the first genes, began to control how it worked inside. From now on inheritance could happen, the process of passing on adaptations from generation to generation, which has continued ever since.

Life arose on earth, and there it remains. No evidence has yet been found for the existence of life anywhere else in the universe. All living things, from every blade of grass to every person, are part of the same process. However it started, we go on living in the only way we can, wondering and questioning and trying to understand, gripped tightly between the dark immensity of space and the inferno not far beneath our feet.

Under the sun

The sun is the closest star to earth. Its light takes a little over eight minutes to reach us. It has become the driving force for life. Without it life would end.

Some 2000 million years ago, single-celled organisms in the sea began to harness the sun's energy, using it to make food. They took in water and carbon dioxide – as a gas from the air – and in sunlight the mixture became a simple form of sugar. As a waste product, they released oxygen into the atmosphere. These cells were the first plants.

At first the oxygen was poisonous to many forms of life, and it destroyed for ever the chemicals in the sea which had allowed life to evolve in the first place. But then something else happened. Some of the oxygen changed to ozone, shielding the earth from most of the harmful, ultra-violet rays of the sun, which had always been able to change genes haphazardly, destroying adaptations. Now life could become more advanced. Soon there were cells which took in oxygen and obtained energy from eating plants. These were the first animals.

Animals depend on plants, as plants depend on the sun. Even meat-eaters like deinonychus depended on plants, because they ate animals which ate plants. In the end, all the energy needed by a baby or a caterpillar, by a nettle or a tree, by a frog, an owl or an aphid, comes from the sun. Some of the energy is passed on each time one organism eats another. Eating anything is like swallowing sunshine.

Life exists on land, in the air and in the sea – but survival is impossible above a certain height or below a certain depth. The zone where life happens, the biosphere, is some 21 km from top to bottom, like a thin film around the earth. In this delicate layer, all the great adventures of evolution have taken place.

The earth keeps changing, and life keeps pace with it. The biosphere is like a kaleidoscope, with each coloured piece a different way of living. One species becomes extinct, but another takes its place, living in a similar way. The kaleidoscope turns, the pattern changes, but the colours stay the same.

When the dinosaurs died, mammals replaced them. Rhinoceroses filled the gap left by the giant plant-eater triceratops, lions and tigers did the hunting instead of tyrannosaurus and deinonychus. No one mourned the death of the last fantastic pterodactyl, and somewhere its body sank away unnoticed. But the air was soon filled with singing birds.

300 million years ago
The first vertebrates on land were amphibians, which returned to the water to breed. Huge dragonflies fluttered through the swampy forests.

100 million years ago
For about 150 million years dinosaurs dominated the world. No one knows for certain why they became extinct.

50 million years ago
Once the dinosaurs had gone, the stage was set for the rise of the mammals. A huge variety evolved, much greater than exists today.

400,000 years ago
Primitive man, armed and cunning, lived in a world of mighty animals. But soon his skill as a hunter brought many of them to extinction.

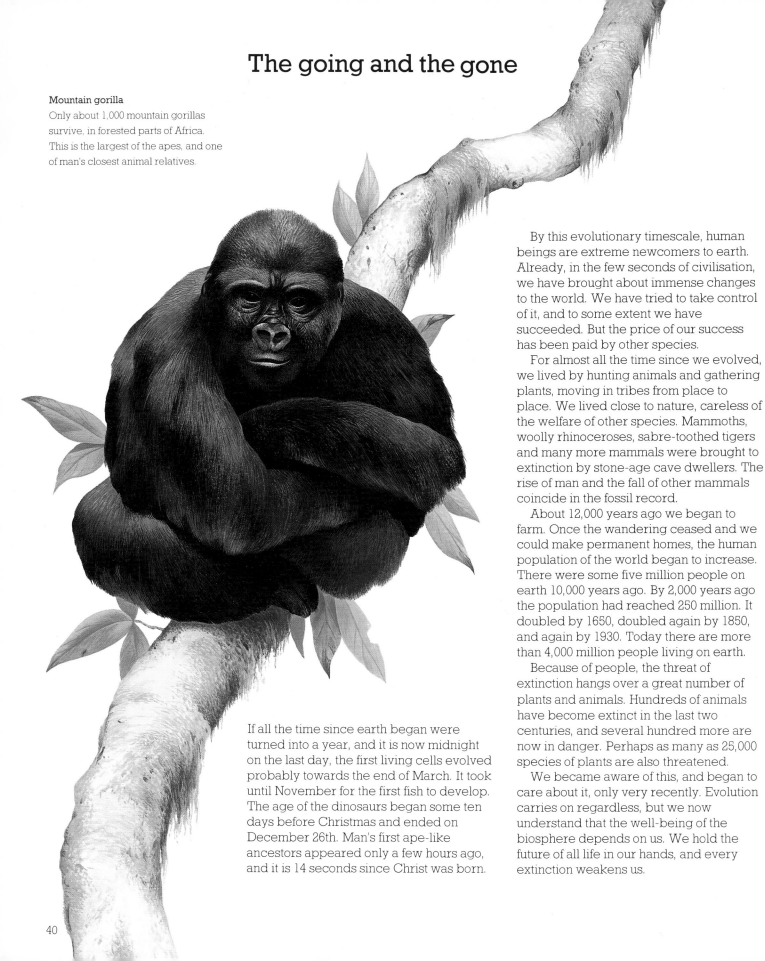

The going and the gone

Mountain gorilla
Only about 1,000 mountain gorillas survive, in forested parts of Africa. This is the largest of the apes, and one of man's closest animal relatives.

By this evolutionary timescale, human beings are extreme newcomers to earth. Already, in the few seconds of civilisation, we have brought about immense changes to the world. We have tried to take control of it, and to some extent we have succeeded. But the price of our success has been paid by other species.

For almost all the time since we evolved, we lived by hunting animals and gathering plants, moving in tribes from place to place. We lived close to nature, careless of the welfare of other species. Mammoths, woolly rhinoceroses, sabre-toothed tigers and many more mammals were brought to extinction by stone-age cave dwellers. The rise of man and the fall of other mammals coincide in the fossil record.

About 12,000 years ago we began to farm. Once the wandering ceased and we could make permanent homes, the human population of the world began to increase. There were some five million people on earth 10,000 years ago. By 2,000 years ago the population had reached 250 million. It doubled by 1650, doubled again by 1850, and again by 1930. Today there are more than 4,000 million people living on earth.

Because of people, the threat of extinction hangs over a great number of plants and animals. Hundreds of animals have become extinct in the last two centuries, and several hundred more are now in danger. Perhaps as many as 25,000 species of plants are also threatened.

We became aware of this, and began to care about it, only very recently. Evolution carries on regardless, but we now understand that the well-being of the biosphere depends on us. We hold the future of all life in our hands, and every extinction weakens us.

If all the time since earth began were turned into a year, and it is now midnight on the last day, the first living cells evolved probably towards the end of March. It took until November for the first fish to develop. The age of the dinosaurs began some ten days before Christmas and ended on December 26th. Man's first ape-like ancestors appeared only a few hours ago, and it is 14 seconds since Christ was born.

Apollo butterfly
The butterflies live high in the Swiss Alps, and can survive intense mountain cold. But they are very rare, and are the first insect ever to be protected under international law.

Blue whale
Hunting brought the blue whale – the largest animal that has ever lived – to the verge of extinction. Now the species is protected, but few remain.

Rafflesia
The largest flower in the world, and now becoming one of the rarest, can be up to 90 cm across, and smells of rotting meat – an adaptation to attract flies.

Polar bear
Though polar bears, the largest Arctic predators, are now protected, many are shot every year, some by trophy hunters, others by Eskimos for food and fur.

In the end

There are so many ways to tell the story of life, to say how life may have started, how it changed and still changes, how you came to be born and how you happened to be what you are. You can look at yourself in a mirror, or at a baby, or at a butterfly, or at a tree in blossom, and somehow the whole story is told again, told to your eyes without words. The longer you think, trying to understand, the greater becomes the sense of wonder. Science offers only part of an answer. In the end there is no complete answer that can be put into words. There is always a space beyond, a silence which you can leave empty, or fill however you like.

Ideas change all the time. It is not long since we thought that the world was flat, or that bonfires lit on earth could increase the strength of the sun. It is not long since we burnt people as witches, or went to wizards or cunning men to be cured of illnesses. We know more now, and we know different things. But we do not know everything. Knowledge is always incomplete, like a journey without end.

Out of incompleteness, out of silence, grows the great richness of ideas, beliefs and faiths which exists in the world. All of these are part of the story. The idea of evolution by natural selection, which is less than 200 years old, does not exclude other ideas, which touch in different, more private ways on the wonder which surrounds us.

Different scientists develop the theory of evolution in different ways. Some propose that evolution happened gradually and slowly, with the little differences adding up one by one to great changes. Others think that there were periods when evolution happened very quickly, with long times without change between them. No one can be certain of the truth.

Hope begins where the questions end. This is a personal truth, a secret way of telling the story to yourself. You think about evolution, about cells, about the way life goes on. But no words can really explain how you sometimes feel when you look at the world, the happiness that comes inside you. No words are necessary for this. There is life and love and hope. When the questions stop, every baby ever born remains what it always was, a miracle.

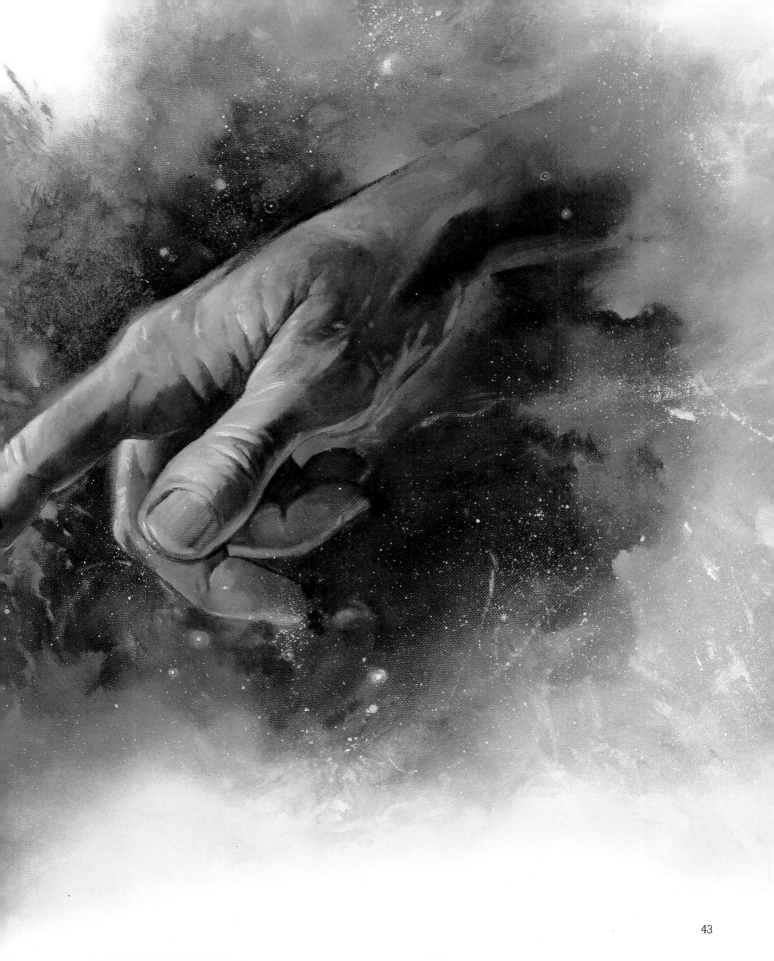

Index

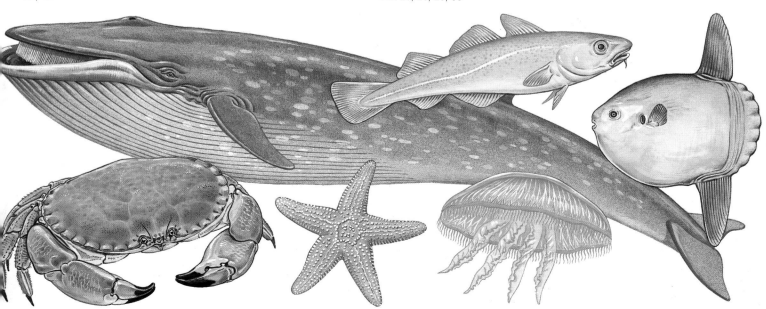

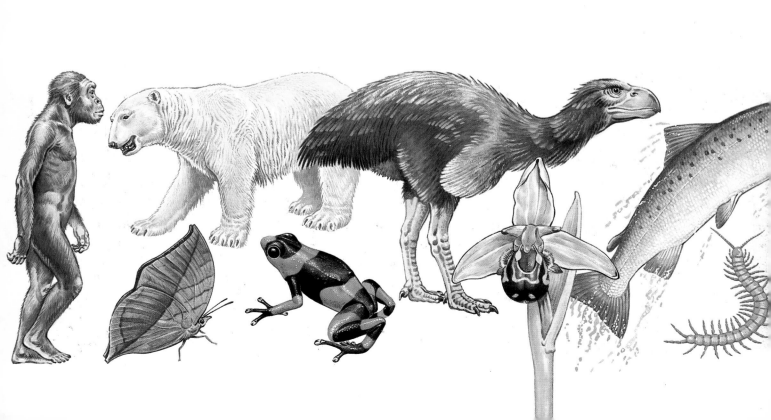